BOOKS BY JULIAN TALAMANTEZ BROLASKI

gowanus atropolis (Ugly Duckling Presse, 2011)

(co-editor) *NO GENDER: Reflections on the Life & Work of kari edwards* (Litmus Press/Belladonna Books, 2009)

ADVICE FOR LOVERS

CITY LIGHTS SPOTLIGHT SERIES NO. 7

JULIAN TALAMANTEZ BROLASKI

ADVICE

FOR

LOVERS

CITY LIGHTS

SAN FRANCISCO

CITY LIGHTS SPOTLIGHT
The City Lights Spotlight Series was founded in 2009, and is
edited by Garrett Caples.

Library of Congress Cataloging-in-Publication Data
Brolaski, Julian Talamantez.
Advice for lovers / Julian Talamantez Brolaski.
p. cm. — (City Lights spotlight ; 7)
ISBN 978-0-87286-581-5
I. Title.
PS3602.R6425A65 2012
811'.6—dc23
2012005505

Cover Image: Johnny Ray Huston, *Palace Wall* (2011) [detail]
Courtesy of the artist and [2nd floor projects].

The editor would like to thank Johnny Ray Huston and Margaret Tedesco for
their assistance with this project.

All City Lights Books are distributed to the trade by
Consortium Book Sales and Distribution: www.cbsd.com

For small press poetry titles by this author and others,
visit Small Press Distribution: www.spdbooks.com

City Lights Books are published at the City Lights Bookstore,
261 Columbus Avenue, San Francisco, CA 94133
www.citylights.com

for
Eddy

ACKNOWLEDGMENTS

Many thanks to the editors in whose journals and collections versions of these poems appear: *580 Split*, *Stolen Island Review*, *Magazine Cypress*, *Boog City*, *Small Town*, *Bay Poetics* (Faux Press, 2006), *Vanitas*, *EOAGH*, *Boog City*, *Jacket*, and *Drunken Boat*. Several of these poems also appear in a chapbook, *The Daily Usonian* (Atticus/Finch, 2004).

Thanks to my friends and early readers of this work: Julia Bloch, Corinne Crawford, Michael Cross, Brent Cunningham, kari edwards, Alison Fenton, Judith Goldman, E. Tracy Grinnell, Robert Hass, Lyn Hejinian, Rodney Koeneke, David Larsen, Nathanaël (Nathalie Stephens), Stephen Ratcliffe, Elizabeth Rosenberg, Cynthia Sailers, Jennifer Scappettone, Dana Ward, Elizabeth Willis, Elizabeth Marie Young, Stephanie Young, the Nudist Course, and many others.

CONTENTS

NUDISMS

NOTES

ADVICE FOR LOVERS

DEDICATION TO VENUS

I am a love poet, and dedicate all my verses to Love, that god among goddesses, goddess among gods, that cavalcade of hearts, that point on which I turn as both thir clerk and thrall, and also thir messenger—therefore herkneth ladings, lordes, if you would love, to these advices.

ADVICES

'You must sit down,' says Love, 'and taste my meat.'
So I did sit and eat. —GEORGE HERBERT, 'Love' (III)

DISCIPULƎ AMORIS

Now hearkneth to me lordings and good lades—
Upcome in a wood of dourful shades,
Who'd be love's scholar, discipulə amoris
Learnt in all the lossom ways that love is
Lernt in that sweet science of bruising
Which renders lewd, so that at your choosing
You may yet plot to snare your pet
Or blaze thir parts in englyssche, or by your very glance
To hook a hating falconet.
Hearken—and you'll spin on proferrments to dance
   Ladings listen, if you would loving prove
   And glorify the lewed, lust and Love.

I AM MY OWN BIG BROTHER

Call me cunt, I am my own big brother,
Like Hesiod, had he had his druthers
I'm spitting on the nail I ought to clip
To make my heart thump harder on the lam.
That rhyming hazard that you *thot* you writ
That fucks folks harder than a free verse can
Is lisping with its colored consonants
Is buggering the fuck out of abstinence,
While my bitch sits high atop the firmament
Tugging at the garter of the god of gods—
& with such look of am'rous compliment
I blushed to voice, flushed to blow thir wad.
   My rhymes, though sometimes given to be shallow—
   Will not their horns unspill, nor pose themselves as fallow.

WHAT TO DO WHEN YOUR MUSE BECOMES YOUR LOVER

A loose tongue
The high Kahuna desert,
Vulnerable to thieves.
Music for trampolines
Secrecy's trappings—
I'm not suffering,
It's just annoying
Like how a tattoo tickles.
You fool, my Muse told me
It appears, in your book
The cure for Love is more love!

ON HOW TO TRANSFORM AN IMAGINARY INTO AN ACTUAL LOVER

I do not want your gratitude I want your panties. —ALLI WARREN

Now all but one citadel is burning. My persuasion is tending to me softly in the Greek letters. How do you theorize Love? If you look closely enough at a word, you'll find it contains its opposite. These are the thieves Achilles reckoned with, one coatcheck down from the Imagination. He looks like a linebacker but he runs like a deer. . . . Many come inside the versification of a cold letter—some prefer numbers. Last night I burned sheets I didn't even know I had. Now all but one cure remains in the city: we're running out of water, getting overrun with water. My dream of your name becomes an embarrassing chant. Many, Cuz, step inside the building once burning and declare it their laugh-riot temple. You know better, having found the cure for Love.

ON HOW TO TRANSFIGURE THE BODY UTTERLY

I practically ran to get out all these lonesome shoes. Shut up inside the shop I was, raging like a bull. Maddened in the middest of the race, reaching more up than across, I saw the gold foil façade of a house built on corpses. Of a sea composed entirely of horses, all running to their death—

> *O I wish to the lord I'd never been born*
> *Or died when I was young*
> *Then I'd never have seen your shinin blue eye*
> *Or heard your lyin tongue*

Into this ugly & haole world was I wakened, the morning star met with its wanderer. *All the good times are past and gone*, this habitat imbred me like a shrive. Be with me always . . . take any form . . . love is like, love is like falconry.

THE REAL

What if I commanded you never to change, stay cool . . .
—STEPHANIE YOUNG

So much easier, violent, to be a man in rain
To be a common man in a dent truck
The rain provoking us to 'Join Arnold'
Our joke politicians, a letter and a cartoon.

You will have many desires and the dream
Of fulfilling the desire will outdo the real.
One in the hand, one
Suffering doubly—to your cause sweethart.
Step up to silver, the San Andreas, the driver is wanton

The very next person you saw from the bus
The very next wet dream in a series
Maybe the /h/ sound is what I'm missing
In the maiden whispering low

See the Real gleams out of its bath
With a chin like Spartacus

Mortal desires, the real
Hand foisting

The real heart, a jest at call
And response. Many break when they would seem
To hang—would a real experiment mean having
No form to feign to fuck?

Oncely among these trifles I am thralled.
Even swans say their concern without a crack in the voice.
Do I leastwise share that brute trajectory?
Enjoyst thou paranoia?

ON HOW TO FEIGN COURTESY

Cum melius foribus possis, admitte fenestra.
(Though it were better by the door, admit them by the window.)
—OVID, *Ars Amatoria* III.605

What are all these ribbons you're hanging yourself by,
whilst adding a third to our private teatime? Your scarf
flutters to the pavement entirely duplicitously, you accidently
address us as Your Excellency. In short,
everything was 'singly and in swarms' (the gentlemen)
or 'singly and in throngs' (the flies).
I've had it with your honeyed words! they *sound* sunny,
who know angels flow so low, etc., but we
are not passing with our astute Prince every evening.
No-no-no. The mouth's agog but the coach is not ready.

ON HOW TO ADDRESS YOUR LOVER

Thug—ebony—lithe! Grand lune,
If I had my way (good gawd)
Let us do our trussing
Let us do our tressing

Hellespontine onna Trojan sibyl
To hold a thorny thing tenderly

O homework
Earthquake explosion
Clodio cum Clodius
Panoche Inn in the badlands

Springolin sprung back
W/ washboard realism
I hear you're feeling poorly,
Well don't weep so sorely

Meum desiderium unicus
Mel meum

Meum dulcis hirundo[1]

My one want
Honey of mine
Sweet swallo—

---

1 Published partly as an aid to teaching Latin conversation, Erasmus of Rotterdam, in *Colloquia Familiaria* (1518), recommends these formulae to lovers ('Greetings my . . . '):
Mea corneliola (my little Cornelia)
Mea uita (my life)
Mea lux (my light)
Meum delicium (my darling, delight)
Meum sauauium (my sweetheart, lit. kiss)
Mel meum (my honey)
Mea uoluptas unica (my only joy)
Meum corculum (my sweetheart, lit. little heart)
Mea spes (my hope)
Meum solatium (my comfort)
Meum decus (my glory)

ON HOW TO BLAZON YOUR LOVER

Forget-me-nots, for god's sake, forget-me-nots. —LARRY KEARNY

This, lovers, you must do if you are to blaze your lover. First, proclaim your mode:

> Call xem knockneed, call xem Diana Presents Greece
> A herm in the stars with a hook in xir hand
> Hold my head honey, the death
> The face I wallow toward
> Heaven's osmotic substance,
> Ends of the Scriven horizon.

Misblaze your lover's hands, call xir eyes sapphire, call xem romanesque if the moments be kinder or fair. When time for honey calls for blazing—then count it, speak your lover fair. Say

> I'm your ponyperson in training
> Dear island of Beauty, dear Prochia,
> If the moments be clear,
> If the moments be cloudy or fair

Though it mean to make my brown eyes blue,
I beg you stay true—don't chide me for feigning.

THE SWEET SCIENCE OF BRUISING

O would that I would brim to be so bold
To swim into that icy throne, decanted
With your crotchless chaps, ruthless to behold.
One pluck of the rib and I'm enchanted,
An odder cor on which to cut my thumb,
I rage as if *I* were the brimming one—
Once punched, a pugilist can ought but pander
As sea-things gnaw and grope to get a gander
At our fenestrated fucking. And soon
Each limb is bruised with urgent scarlet moons,
Our brains confound with kisses, and our tongues
Cant to poles of melting candy, your guns
  Blazing to fuck me on the Grykysshe sea
  One leg toward Russia, the other Galilee.

SONG OF SONGS

Stay me with flagons, comfort me with apples, for I am sick with love.
—Song of Solomon, 2.5

Your lips are like tulips your teeth are like doves
Honey my prowess I take as it comes.
Beyond your lip, the golden falcon plunges
Past the long shining neck to your nipples.
All sweet with liquefaction the chest undoes
Itself, my ocean, teased apart with ripples.
Your ass is like a cut pomegranate
Exposing its berry fruit. I can't fit
My fist inside your rosebud, but your kissing,
Darling, so confounds my sodden lip I
Make unto my longings one sweet end. Things
Caught in the treetops oft increase their eye
 Toward wandering, but I confess that I
 Sometime for sake of doughty rhyme must lie.

DEEP IMAGE: TO VENUS

Eels caught bright-eyed in the rafters. —ELIZABETH MARIE YOUNG
Horses gleaming and healing in the white sun. —GARY SNYDER

What horse went gleaming, headlong and guffing,
What ghost went wheezing, purple and chuffing?
None. Meanwhile the ants are fat on the fat,
Lugging the cakelet. The wind moored after that.
To the bateauiste juggling the rigging
Confounding the sailor w/ chest ringing—
I send my song. I lost my joie de vivre
And so I sing this—since I hate to live.
Venus, it's so unruly of the sheep
To fuck me in the ass instead of sleep.
Why don't you come *here* from out your grotto,
And take me in the front, and make our motto
   Let's this or that, let's hard and then let's harder,
   Beast at my back, Love at my garter.

HOW TO FASHION INTO SPEECH

The cup of orbit, I am fain to drink, w/ you anear. Will you have me fashion into speech? Echoes of Black Friday on Wallstreet, an invitation to a meeting of the minds at Stephen Hawkings', idiopathic cell growth. Water from that height is not something soft you fall into. Rough trade plays square, angel—going to work by one shot of a cold laser, stars to you when we're almosting midnight. I carried colored pens and stars to doctor my standing-only invitation. More than the fictitiousness of the sea, that french kissed me, and left. If the shoreline was a trompe l'œil, would I have the sense to look for a soft place to fall?

THE PERFECT LOVE POEM TUTORIAL

*There's a place in the Antarctic that scientists refer to straightfaced
as the Doldrums.* —J. P.

Are you about to leap into the Aegean, thou blackheart, you dasher
of ascots? Do you have the doldrums, a stillness on the sea? Do you
wish you could write love poems which magnify your woes? Perhaps
looser still with your hibitions? One etymological halo of light, one
fox in the snow. Love poetry is about knowing your references. Now
all but one citadel is burning . . .

Will I accept the dedication?—my goodness! These are just the
working notes for part of an *impression* of my acceptance, my dear,
which you may not term a confession. But I can't find anything in the
doldrums I recognize—is our encounter macabre—am I the brack-
ish person, the ear of a squid? Either way my ink jets blackly—I'm
not hauled out of any river. Island, atrium, you're floating in the
weblog you decry, you're baptized in barnyards high and dry, or as
Kasey says, things get completely butch.

The *poetic* function is non-sequitorial: an awareness-of-the-
message-for-its-own sake. What's to be communicated *there*, my
little earlobe? The *phatic* function is just asserting that language
is really there, 'a profuse exchange of ritualized formulas . . . with

the mere purport of prolonging communication.'[2] Birds are phatic when they tweet, and so are babies when they gurgle at you. Dorothy Parker has a good example of it:

> *'Well,' the young man said. 'Well!' she said. 'Well, here we are,' he said. 'Here we are,' she said, 'Aren't we?' 'I should say we were,' he said, 'Eeyop! Here we are.' 'Well!' she said. 'Well!' he said, 'well.'*

Therefore harry and fret yourself as a habit. When bronze is cold comfort in these reindeer games, mouth the words of our national anthem—Love—where it hurts most, don laurels and olive garlands. If you hear a song you like, come and rent a girl or guy. Say, I'm your ponyperson in training. I saw and I approved the gleaming wing.

---

2   Roman Jakobson, 'Closing Statement: Linguistics and Poetics.'

I KNOCKED ALL TALES

I, the sultan of these vast purple props,
I'm displaying my affection full view of the street.
Could glaciers hide me from my Love, from my own tears?
I knocked all tales to the nerdiness of forms,
That forested heart committed to the mails.
Could clouds deface one, waxing wond'rous proud
From thir own taut, from thir own tautless face?
Could we begin like a glacier, melting,
When even th'Antarctic is melting—why
Should we stay each other's side of the border?
Nay, we reduplicate in scribal error
You'd know them too, Pauli Shore meets Gertrude Stein,
A kiss not kosher—good thing there's two of you.
You could pray a whole godlaughing divine
With Parton's painted locks, and yet how worthy
I find the catty mastress in thir prime. How can I pet
To pardon you, leaving my accoutrements behind?

Your flesh will yield like tomato before too long—
Displaying its affections full view of the street,

Where the salt-meats go with the longness of my tales and tongue
And the riverbanks are gone-gone, and the starlets,
Like pears, remind us we are curvaceous.
Nothing but cleavage and clouds, your habits
Prickle the opposite—instead of riding
Rodeo, there's mutton bustery and turrets.
Did I lurch, bending the acrostic moment full tincturely?
Que sera, sera sera sera.
This isn't a heart I heart to heart, heart
But merely a walk I seek to ambulate.
Mister, here's a bag with all my money,
You're a wrastler in a city known for its fog,
I cannot envy you until you bud. I'm displaying my affections
Full view of the street. Das Vandaya, old playground!
In my youth I was too perfect for you.

ALOHA CUM YAKUZA

Faze the field that fellates thir messiah
Phrase the frets that foment jambalaya
Force the fiends to leave off penetralia—
Having no form to feign to fuck, Arnaut,
Is swimming gainst the heels.

Do they find some math in it?
Some face, some fondling with tailgates
Gunning lordily? No wrought iron bed
Upsets the tum, nothing misleads the wrists:
Nothing fails in the proportion.

Fight for fags to fuck the sleek regalia
Flummox the fleet that fondles our Gaspara
Flout the furs that feed off la stile nuova
That there's no form to feign to fuck, Arnaut,
Is filching us for meals.

The bruised topoi are arranging
The furniture again. Lost in the shoals

Of a notion, she could no longer be called
Anytime Annie. Check it out,
An attestation of penetralia!

Flout the fakes that feed off marginalia
Fjord the few that figment automania
Feud with fevers fawning on aphasia—
To feign—not to fuck a form, Arnaut,
Is making shoddy deals.

Popularity is naught but mathematical
Persuasion, midst lashings
Bout the ankle—Aloha cum yakuza.
Metrists use the poet
To go about their math.

Is it a murmmurring of that hell
Causes me to sleep causes me to wake?
Ornamentalia: a burnout mummery,
A plume of somnambulist plastic,
Before, during, and after the tortures.

BA BA AUBADE

Listen, it's not like pettiness calls off the kissing—it's the SUN, you fool! Chiffonery is not liberated by death, but in death a kind of prose, a prosaic rest, instead of frankly stealing pastorals. If I am exposed to the tremulous leaves, do I commit myself to the flowering? Why when taking a cab must I make frank use of my handkerchief? The floorboards are glittered with beeswax, I am *for* this beautiful crossing of the pines, and the words I had with them fairly pitch on the hour.

The price of kissing Keats—to whom I affect a certain smoothness of mind, and the mediocrity of love. To whit, my darksome peach-pit! No sugartongued sap to tell me how badly I am outnumbered, he often flips abundantly the air. Please surr, he is a genius with his tendril locks. Sate your hard heart with madeira and be ladylike. Lily B cursed for having music but no wit, already the cauldron of my brain drinking in the idolatrous papery, miniature weddings, sundry storms and like familial episodes. Hir nerves and total recall in ink-pot terms. I hazard the sanguinary ducks and drakes of the dawn—I guess legally I am blind.

THE ART OF LOVE AS CONVERSE

Why so insistent upon the polyglot, my friendly friendly? Why be charmed by /w/s? It's just a party bowed under the radar. Will I place the pearls before me? No but you're givin me an idea.

We were caught amidst the seven Roman hills, flicking the burning ember to a parched throat. Do I detect a note of jealousy for our dandified companion? That is both hilarious and endearing. As you know I am a sucker for the juice, and my hearts are polyglot, my hearts . . .

But why do I court the spoken-for ships? Ever since you said you never wrote love poems I have secretly made your empire my business to conquer. Don't tell me I paid the stage on its polar nights! I begged to get you *on* the stage, I roused bears from their wintry sleeps!

But soon I realized the true art of love is not in kissing but in conversation. Well, it is in kissing. It is in conversation. But the mouth is such a cavalier renegade what insists on sucking hellspont, and so the desire for love remains unfulfilled. The third of this partite is Love, which solidifies the first two functions—(dative and vocative) the given-to and the calling out.

Your letter, Antonius, a touch, and two kisses on the balcony. But we're not in Monrovia! Your ends, so heavily stopped, berate this touch as an exile sloughing off its *Tristia*. Ovid on the Black Sea, far from Rome. The error, probably Corinna, betakes itself to the sea where minerals suck at the sun lapping at our ears.

Where I espied *you*, marigold, all gold like Hermes on the loam, ascending the Olympian mount, wings at your feet and at your wings. Thanks for having a hand at my form—beauty suffuses. What moribund bouquets are we become! Here's glot for you: algolagnia.[3] For the wind puffs our smoke so high there's never any private . . . even Webster has lost its license for the lexicon . . .

---

3 Either masochism or sadism; algos (Greek 'pain') + lagneia ('lust').

TO A RIVAL (PARIS, BEGGING BOY)

Florēat sea things who would break the balls
Of fucking flirty princes, next to nonce.
Such whimsiat is bled in bellows,
And begging while I buss his hawkling's ponce.
How can I loathe that little libertine?
His hands are like pansies his teeth are like tombstones—
Soon he'll be decked in dreary bombazine
And dialing-a-fuck with his moonstones.
Beside that closet queen, you're thalassic,
Bluejacket, your festive gestury upcatches
The creamy nymphs: the illusion phatic.
Me and the bitches are packed and matchless—
Bellicose hothead, too much of lechery
Spells duel, so hang your surly chivalry.

HOW TO BRAG TO YOUR LOVER

I can get more women than a passenger train can ha-aul.
—JIMMIE RODGERS, 'Blue Yodel #1'

Lordy, I've had it with your cruel habit
To leash me bout the neck with sundry gambits
But refuse to lead, so I'm left dragging
Round this leather, but got noperson bragging
Of what a prize brat they bagged. Go flagellate
Late schoolkids, leave me here to ambulate
The docks at dawn, prowling for a merperson.
I'll get more play than Porfirio can
A lolly in every pocket, it's on—
Don't think I'm sitting waiting for your call
I got action from here to the Caspian
I couldn't care if you call me at all.
   I got ones to love me well beyond their means
   And some to feel me up by gossiping streams.

ON INVECTIVE OR THROWING SHADE

Not from the haters do your fellows lurch
Mooning across plateaus of purloined pitch
Once gianted by midnight on its perch
Now preening their tailcoats, milked, breederish
Like fishmongrelled Mary, honing downward
On salty cads who salt for forlorn take.
Go spend the ire you think your posy's conquered!
Heart-dotters, webloggers, slammers—eat cake
And if you can, come suck my goodly cock.
Poets, poetasters, you can't freak to Frank
Can't choliambic with that limping walk
No ass without the hassle's shooting blanks,
   But severally swinging what disgust—
   You fix your sentiments on myth or bust.

THE SWEET SCIENCE OF BRUISING IN FOAMY GREEK (THE POET CURSES LOVE)

You gave me sweet bruisings enough, my friend
And now, we drink! Hot noon, my ass was handled
You bucked me and broke me round the bend
Until my luckiest hair was tangled.
O now, turtledove, dostow oppose me?
Gosh, ignosco tibi, you were all candy,
Candid, honey, candy, and most subtilly!
And now you dally more than any dandy
Tupped in a tight embrace—now doctis
Is your labor writ, now you're spoken for.
I'll tell you muhfuckers what *Love* is
It courts your cork and then it dims the door
   While you hang there in a savage chastening
   With nary a hustler to do your hastening.

WHAT TO SAY UPON BEING ASKED TO BE FRIENDS

Why speak of hate, when I do bleed for love?
Not hate, my love, but Love doth bite my tongue
Till I taste stuff that makes my rhyming rough
So flatter I my fever for that one
For whom I inly mourn, though seem to shun.
A rose is arrows is eros, so what
If I confuse the shade that I've become
With winedark substance in a lover's cup?
But stop my tonguely wound, I've bled enough.
If I be fair, or false, or freaked with fear
If I my tongue in lockèd box immure
Blame not me, for I am sick with love.
    Yet would I be your friend most willingly
    Since friendship would infect me killingly.

ON HOW TO LEAVE YOUR LOVER

Dear laurding of the lyre, let's out of here—
I've pricked with posies ere I got my drear
From your incantive mouth, my moonstruck pilgrim.
You don't move enough your mouth in hymn
To limn our bodies as they lilting swirl
Toward amrous Arden, to despite the curl
That makes them say we're savage. Take this lock
That lisps of argosies, say a sad song
To send at least our spinnets from the dock
And right this trysta with no further wrong.
Then retreat, Cuz, into your self-made cave
And fold this token with the toys I gave
   Inside your strongest box, and do not look
   Fondly on lines I will no longer brook.

SONGS OF LOVE OF GRIEF

Correctness in Love, as in English, is something to move toward but never reach—its horizon continually vanishing. Love is an elaborate set of rules cut off from the secretarial pool. It's Alexander Pope, ringing his bell in the middle of the night, suffering the sudden onslaught of a couplet. Endeared to get the slough out of my brain, my slovenly brother, spit-in-my-eye. 'Goddess! Nymph! Perfect! Divine!' says Lysander, when he's crazy with the juice. Why do lovers constantly speak of their lover's eyes? It's the humid beams they rapturate, it's the vaporous tears they drink in place of sex, it's the juice and its antidote . . .

My wanton-locked friend, in Shakespeare love is glossed as 'superficiality, absoluteness, irrationality.' No vapid manual darkening your doorstep, no magma. A number of diarists pinpoint this middling moment and call it Terpsichore—who delights in the dance—who deigns not smear a letter. They say you can enter the blues at any point, & the wingèd word is the one that accomplishes its mission. Your sweet skin's sacred fruit, I trow, causing me to lean heavily over the table. . . . Vile is how Helena thinks, ugly as a bear. Its defeatures making me to wonder whether the love juice actually *worked*.

ON NOT BEING ABLE TO PERCEIVE ANGELS

in the twilight lo
I stood before the twilight
without even a moon
jacking up the artifice
the proverbial number of angels
that could fit on the head of a pin
before whom, and in what habit
I speak—stop me at the very
vestibule and rip up my ticket
one frosty address will not
diminish one jott my vegetable love

NUDISMS

Take off your clothes and say procedure. ——TAYLOR BRADY

INVOCATION TO SPICER: SIMILIA SIMILIBUS CURANTUR

My purse, my person, my extremest means / Lie all unlock'd to your occasions. —WILLIAM SHAKESPEARE (Antonio to Bassanio, *Merchant of Venice* I.i.141-142)

> Whatever it was, Spicer thought
> he could do it. I can't say ship
> without wanting it to wreck.
> My map skills
> fled for an argonaut
> whilst sad songs
> basically bleed cash.
>
> No-one in America is a poet
> for a living, and Rome
> is a city in Georgia
> as well as our terrible legacy.
>
> Like Paul Célan saying
> I would regale you with snow,
> magic become desire

on the open throes
in the mouth of spring
by a literal lake the dog
drops the tennis
ball gingerly in
constructs for it
a moat.

To what do we dare/owe
this desire?
An obviate oracle
a leaflet with its hooks.

The north and the south pole
are the points from which
all directions on earth are figured.
Jack and his dying. Between
the tropic of cancer
and the arctic circle
you were headed
for a beauty contest in Berkeley.

Your mind's tossing on the ocean
sometime tomorrow with your ships.
Jack, can't you see how sad songs
help when you're sad?

THE ORPHIC NUDE

In our past senses no sarcophagi. Aardvark do eat up experiences, weeping in front of the CEO. To jump the bones of a mummy is debatable, the nocturne shapeshifting to include less a sickle than a cycle. Whoever sells my secrets will die a flowery death, and I'm not kidding. For at least three reasons I refuse to take such a foolish memo. My favorite hyacinth, with the missus in the gutter. Phallic in overall form, labial in detail, the tearful caveperson—capable of smelling colors.

RICKY MARTIN ON HOMOSEXUALITY

You don't survive a love letter from me.

What is beyond calculus? It is a young man's world where the
genius is a physics major, a star at eighteen.

You can put my poster on the wall and think of it however you
want.

When you finally stop taking math classes . . . it's lonely to be the
only poet-scientist.

With great learning, you can outdo Dostoevsky.

In this business you deal with so much fantasy. You must find
the anti-ship, that which disintegrates the ship, namely the
submarine.

When it comes to love, you cannot pull a whip on your own self.

I was saturated—I didn't know what I liked, I didn't know what I
hated.

FUCK ME HARDER

Fuck me harder, leave the haters behind
As you know I am a slut for leisure
Arrest me on the mountaintop's incline,
For I've klepted when I ought to please your
Neglected epic skin, and pull your hair.
When the people call my pigtails prairie
Step in, honey, and set the aspect square
Put me in a suit and call me Mary,
Transcoping this goy's grist or that one's scope.
Holy monogram, how you like to tease,
Tender cufflink, I'm hurting for the grope
That sets my alpha at its churlish ease.
    So strap me to the bed and knife my garter
    Until I'm screaming baby fuck me harder.

SONG IN THE SHADE

How shaded you are in the vine, Calvus,
And yet you think our verses will upbraid
And, cataractous, be the death of us?
You see how keen on carbon copies I'm uplaid,
All unctuous against the slavish numbers,
Lit glancingly, I doggedly elide
If only to broach, my sometime counter,
The sea that barters its clock for candor.
Who walks that way, like Cypress in the wind?
To Italy with that monstrous villainy
That crowns our arbus with a sea-thing's fin.
Yet how breezy you are, in the mutiny
    I hear Tubas—the glosses are runic
    The light makes dapples all along your tunic.

AMOROSA ERRANZA

Cosi mi trovo in amorosa erranza.
(Thus I find myself an errancer in love.)
——DANTE

All my dark hardiments begin, so furious and so fell. All disarrayed in love I began to speak of Mariners. And when I saw the grove divided into double parts, which ways I took, diversely can I tell but can no ways *devise*. So in I enterred was, and marvelled at the wandering way. Although my leman, I am in wondrous doubt —tell me, ERE I DIE OF LOVE—which way to turn? Your hands are like pansies your teeth are like tombstones, and all along the way even the labyrinths shuddered. Where can I go to powder my nose safely? Your address makes me feel intimate, yet I undergo the strangest beguilements, I become incredulous.

RIME

(AFTER GASPARA STAMPA)

You know who was first
Meat to the Trojans, thus to you—
Upon that walk I ambulate,
Never supressing my intention

High in Hollister
Or walking the dog in Kailua
All ends in you,
Nothing else is.

Darling, I'd eat the sun
If it meant
What I want it to mean
Ships long crashing are not

As desolate as my swiss cheese heart
And in and out slides wormy
Regret, what makes
A meal of me.

YEAR OF THE MISFIT

Dear envelope the feeling,
That I have sealed
To the writing of no more letters—
Fate to thee, fate to the fish

Of my heart, they are reading
A religious pamphlet, it is
Covered in golden scales
And how many would come

To the blackboard
To write such greek?
Someone took the blue couch
And took to the finish like

Horses poked and prodded
Running for the good of horses,
Itself yoked to the desert-as-moon
And stretches its long neck

The sunset provoking
Our tenderest aspect, *they*
Were here, here they were
There they went.

And all the meantime
We rant against the devil's herd.
Who said there was a coast
That even Marilyn could interject?

OPEN LETTER FROM THE LIBERTINE

Mes amicae,

You profess love, you profess deviance, but do you get dirty? Nope, I'm stuck at second base, and barely holding on. I'm looking for Venus inna burningpitchfork, I'm scenting my body with myrrh. O-wilt-thou-leave-me-so-unsatisfied? My loves were never passing through the joyous hurly hours . . . such as this . . .

O horsefall of the quickening sundown—dear rider, they argue I am in love with love—not so. Still I can speak on both sides of the question—I can find equivalences where there never were . . . I can take a paramour and make them worthy, tho they are prudish. I can love both fair and brown, except I wax lame—I circumambulate the dreary sea w/ a bum leg, moaning for my lost Laura. My lovers never say to me, let's get heavy and wet our whistles down upon the grain. They are nothing but letdowns.

Brute hearts, betake thyselves to the noons half-lit by shades! Get off or get gone!

Your,
Pet.

FAGGOT LOVE SONGS

He parambulates with parasol
You can't account for such supernova

Buggering the one heaven
You set your sights on.

Young O with his livery
Young O w/ his distress

Having emerged on the other side of desire
Having said jew
Having said faggot love songs

Machine that vexes, as the ironclad
'Pressing engagement'
This carmine aphrodisiac's a must!

Chatty, not too far gone, young O measures his hips.
What pressing to this engagement!
What aggravated lips!

NOBAUDE

I left you last evening without the usual privileges. A lot of what my body was was toxin, that held me aloft in idle price, far from the witless wood and Arcadia. There's no more moon for birds to buss at over streetlamps. Urchins make their way in the mist, trolling for dinner rolls. How frugal my recent times were spent, the clocks keeping how stoned a content. There'll be much better dawns than this forthcoming.

Now—silver morning, body trussed across a sphere—what would Salome do? *A certain Grace is coming toward you and xe is lovely.* The troposphere might solder the iron we sought here, the sky is neither an abaude.

What Portia lacks is not anatomical, but philosphical: 'bitter is my sustenance, melancholy my food, sorry my wine.' Expressive geometrics of the New York sissy—and with such a disfunctional phone! Portia tells her students get thee to a muhfuckery, where I'll lay thee fool across my lap.

P meets Sally's longings, her shoes untied, and everything about her demonstrating a careless desolation, a blue eye and sunken. *Take one step further and the Grace coming toward you is Beauty. The Grace turned away from you is Restraint.* Hassan pleading for her life, fainting, having a bucket of water thrown on her, reviving.

Nothing but a farce, we animate Wall and Moon. The art is cruxy to the love-juice. Once there was many a sight, but now they are wilting, poor lambs. Once a malapert downpour, uncharacteristic of the rains of this place. Next football, a hemistich. The belle lettrist's idea of a billet-doux, the scientist's idea of a sauna.

What with their consummate barbeque wines, their tawdry dance moves, their go-go girls of yesteryear—we thought the Impressionists were trying to impress people. Fez—an impossibility the universe grew out of. Flaubert saying, Madame Bovary, c'est moi. Loretta casting her lots.

EATING TH'ASTEROID

I didn't see nothin to want or t'unwant. —BOB DYLAN

O prisoner of love, lift up your tatters
Of creams and apricots and punctured feathers—
And darling, turn your wits to country matters.
Let Nina croon and keen to stormy weathers
Let's drink a draught of brandy in the dark.
That one with thir tawdry arrow, Philip
With his trewand pen. Sweet, I dip you dip
We dip, from the formal to Venezia
From the faux to the photorealistic.
Cupid spat more paint than did my sweet Lucretia
Who brushed the corner of my collar with lipstick.
   But I don't care for such unlearnèd bitches
   For they can't ease th'enallage that itches.

HATERZ GOSSIP

And I'll be settin seperate plays, / So on all these separate days, /
Your legs can go they separate . . . ways . . . —USHER

Open your legs when I tell you to, cuz,
For the haters gossip all over town
You got the hottest legs in all the biz
Ride me downtown chauffeur, I'm getting down
On my knees to suck you off, ah fuckoff
W/ your hot self & blow me on the couch
Your tongue is tangling up my careful coiff
To say nothing of your salty-sweet crotch.
Why be chaste upon the ponderous page?
Let's haste for Arden as the beacon wanes
And cream until the darkened ambit's won
Where tree nymphs pay no homage to the sun,
  But languish in a cave, and fainting say
  Your legs, dear cuz, will go their separate ways.

COUNT YCLEPT
(FROM *The Royal Notebook*)

Harrying the lovers to make a diversion in its favor, the Count, having entered Normandy proudly on its mettled charger, recrossed the Sarthe, a groaning cripple on a litter. The objects for the confessional are all taken from where it had a vision in Queens. Norell on mink has the smell of old money. What good is all this mummery to the deep thinker? To summon me is not to be my master. Still, was that train in the film or a sound in the room? There is in the world of maquillage much orange. Wherever it might chance to turn its eyes, the choppy heroic moment, the luxury of wanting.

POEM IN WHICH THE LOVER IS ADDRESSED

Ow Bimkin,
You're taut for sure,

My little pinwheel
You thug-eye I brink

To the mirth of grief
And other zeugmas.

Thou lunate singer
Beauty's door

Blues song that
Crackles, Diana

Begets Greece.
Laura Riding's

Dear Possible,
Caravaggio's angel,
Callimachus' swan,

Antony, Dido, Vincent,
Sebastian, Beatrice
And Naiobe all in tears,

The most perfectly
Shaped tears, like little

Colored orbs. Thou
Devonshire-within-reach

You filthy gadabout
Endearinger than a cuscus

Thou diver with a miner's
Attitude about birds.

HELEN EXCLUDED FROM HEAVEN

You are—different weather in this tropic
One that is jarredness, correctness
Gwyneth is doing Sivvy all wrong
Being the Wife of Bath
The blood on hir neck ensures our safety
A tea I've never since tasted
Under the date palms, smoke
The stuff of roses
The whole in a dark decorum
The map in a musical setting
Making the tavern
To break with the tappester
Persuading us to marry in the margins
This tropic defeats me to my knees
Calling the collossus caw
Pleases the royal
What dips its head for fruits
More godly contempt
More's the pleasure

DIDO TO AENEAS HAVING LEFT THE CAVE

But heark me, m'adam, despite my duller tongue
That I may ease my victory with oil
That you may lap up all my tears for fun
And count my ass among your booty's spoils.
I'm fondling miself to please you now,
Though you be far, and hast'ning on the loam
Toward snow, your presence-absence makes me bow
And bend my brain for ways to bring you home.
If only your chest would breach my waiting lips
I'd trace along your back my dirty secrets,
I'll have you panting while I stroke my whip
And begging while I idly lift my dress.
   I'd slash my braids upon the mart to barter
   If only you'd come home and fuck me harder.

IN THE WAKE OF THE GLEAMING HINDENBURG

I've been to podunk, and the infinitesimal walkthrus, but here's the snake eating its own tail right in front of you. They say we're a waking giant, but the skin's pre-occupied with its scars and garters and its own fraudulent timing. I post between hither and thither with you reading the perfect love poem tutorial.

I listened across the west wing . . . it is now possible to freeze light, if only for nanoseconds. This gesture marks me for a fever pitch. We're on our way to the lilting rubble of Baghdad, we speak of shots, handless, our sighs saltier, bombs undone.

On the tailgate your shadow draws littoral air. In the wake of the gleaming Hindenburg, the shock of the good dear blue over our heads. Dear Liza, would you know me for an aerial thing? Let's this or that. Now I'm cavalier there's no light or air between us.

THE PHILISTINE SMITTEN

Bien sur j'arrive
I take this carrison teemly
Et tomber—ort—there was no open vision
Phineas is dead and the ark of gawd is taken
Tombez sur nous
They brought about the ark of the dead to us
Also my surr hey xe
Plagues were sent
Ark
Philistines
Tres-pass offerings
Idolatrous priestessez
And Dagon upon its face
Xe is my shepherd, and shall perform all my pleasure
Then we shall begin to say to the mountains, fall on us

SIBYL SONG AT TROY

My tell-tale Orpheus, what sibyl could
Hazard apart the reins of rings-that-could—
What dark saturn would lash apart the lance
To trade its goblin for that lush expanse?
Except your darkling eye my lip ascends
Upon the loomèd loam ever so bizarre
All Troy would bend its knees, and rend its greaves
To lean upon that lustrous cheek. Greek star
Of blooming chest, come beat my stardust on
A cocaine mirror, flushed with leaves and all
And freaking on the couch. Brad was well-hung
But does he have the cock, th'erotic gall

    To come until the cocks croon morning's come,
    Crowing like cows until the mornings come?

A GLORIOUS ARRAY OF DIPHTHONGS
SUDDENLY EXTENDS MY EVENING

When my pen is permitted to be discarded, that's when Belinda gives up her lock. Come to my city of siblingly love, where nary a Madonna or an insomnia will recommend us to the hucksters, where the peanut and cotton farmers ponder their own ruin in rain-soaked Georgia or congested Kaintuck, where we court th'illicit soddeneyeds for their backhands. We were striving for a piece of true-love-hair t'encoil w/ our billet-doux, but kept getting left stranded at second base. Would we approach with our scissors, getting negligible with /au/s and /aɪ/s? Just another crazy in love with Love, and it thought it had differentiated itself from its compatriots! Your jealousy, Clodiə, is intolerable—

> It doesn't know how to speak non-erotically
> Immeshed upon its love notes for dear life

Was I inviting/recanting? I'm showing everyone your letters and my irresponse—don't you like the dash and ellipse? Nay, heart, make your Greeks withdraw to helenback—I'm suffering like video stores since ***flix.

THE WHEEL OF SHEEP

I shall be the one to judge between sheep and sheep. —Ezekiel 34.22

Sheep among the tendrilled ivies
Show their posy matter, a cutter's diamond
And a prison window.
Below the tendril shadow
A sheep called the matter ill.

Sheep illin sans herder
Sheep ravaging the larder—
It all hung like spilled blood
In the trilling moment.

Sheep illin sans herder
Sheeplings indicted for murder
And later found
To be too young to punish.

Sheep watch Shirley get sexy drunk and strip
Shirley strips out of xir sheep suit
Shirley going at xir buttons

Amidst fervent bleatings
Untying all xir laces, Shirley
Doing something drunk and sexy.

Sheep tangle till even Yahweh
Cannot tell sheep from sheep.

Sheep undoing the garter
Sheep essaying their shears for barter
Until soon the shepherd with thir mandrake
Nips all bleating in the bud—
A woolen hush descends on the revellers.

LOWING THE LAY

go ferly forth, swete amis
to your amiloun ywis
sheep at slaughter
dreadful of the larder
impressed you

friend or lover,
the court's excesses
whites, pinks and reds
bubbling with largesse
sweetmeats and squashes
cakes and cakelets

friend or lover, why
should we even
think of the dawn?
we only stroll abundantly
we only troll, hey nigh despair

lolling the lay of the land
lulling the lo, lullay lullay
lilting the lo, the lull, the lay,
lulling the lay of the land.

go ferly forth, swete amiloun
to your amis, bliss and boon
above even the silver moon
your kisses take you ywis

barons unbuckling in the noon
& barkeeps arranging their boots
all for the lo, lullay lullay
all for the lure of the land

the lo of the land, lullay lullay
the langoring lull of the land
lowing the lo, the lull, the lay
lulling the lay of the land

NAUTITORIUM

This week a troubled teen in paramilitary garb sets the stage for a host of subtler, smarter enticements. It's the string and the kite and the labyrinth and Icarus. It's just more adrift, they have proved it with monkey studies. I am a visitor to this tenthouse, displayed by way of affection. This scenario, needless to say, the reason you lurk around at bullfights. I am in a kind of Spain. Playing a scene of the zero-zeroes, I am quaking to the core, I am losing to the shining Turk. What would your pose be here? To be occasional, like a diary, stuck on northwest. Merely waking should release some part of me usually closed for the construction. You are of two minds on the question of what to see: *Mummies are lovely but they are gone people*. What does the breath advise, crazy berated thing? I want them gone by morning.

COMPLAINT OF EURYALIS TO THE LADIES OF LEISURE

Euryalis taking leave of Lucretia, precipitated her into such a love-fitte that she ghosted. —Sir Philip Sidney, *Arcadia*

> Doctus et leporus es, my dim moravian king
> What lethargy employed for anarchy, what
> Locust amid the ruins, o costly shepherd,
> What gemmed idol—Jesus or Mahoun—
> Accosts you sharply?
> Doctus et leporus es, my dim moravian king.
>
> To lack the thing I love, how is't possible?
> To wrest upon the counterfact urn
> To limn the posies we suppose among,
> To lay as counter-posy might,
> And come up sugary in the fields
> To lack the thing I love, how is't possible?
>
> All unctious with the savage unguents—
> Does not faction pose with liquefaction on't?
> Asweat with numbers, away on an alchemist's habit?

What then, that I was forward going,
From the very day I broke this brim
All unctious with the savage unguents?

Having foresworn sight
For I ne'er saw true symmetry
Till that night truly
Without lying I swear, withouten lesyng
Having foresworn sight.

That might mean, you gadabout, you edge on mean,
I'm sparking tender for you, churl, can't
You see the floodgates?
Your leopard stalks me there,
Bellowing among the grist and grease.
That might mean, you gadabout, you edge on mean.

But why not love me dear, beyond your means?
Why not feel me up by the silvery stream?

THE REAL, PURCHASED ON CREDIT, DOES NOT LIE BACK

One is spitting teeth out a car window. We make no traffic with our nicety. I thought the postal truck was *in pursuit* of me, ere it made the most of my morning. This is the True West—the fatal jewel of double-blindness:

> *Come, come, Nerissa, for I long to see*
> *Quick Cupid's post that comes so mannerly.*

The Real, purchased on credit, does not lie back, or lie in wait upon perfumed pillows, wrestling all points of suspension, committing the usual architectural travesties: love of the superstructure, love of a well-trained slave. However it—the nudism—is felt more readily in a fever, signifying that the real 'concludes' with mutability. Johnny Cash dreaming of Mexican trumpets, the name horizon stopped. Before I knew it, I had my detector. Nudism at land's end. With a name like Pacifica, where'd you think they'd unveil it?

MY LOVE OF THE SILVRY THIGH

(AFTER ANDRÉ BRETON'S 'FREEDOM OF LOVE')

A beaky pinch and drink me, little steeple —MELISSA BENHAM

My love of the silvry thigh, whose
Limbs of cautionary limbecks smooth
Make moonlight of its minions' manners
And cause those churlish sprites to stammer
A beaky pinch and drink me, little steeple
Till love-licour demands a droughty earful.

My love it's-always-darkest-before-dawn
My love o bod, aubade the moon is down
My love obeyed the tender lappe what
Wells I suck, ink of lording posy's gut
Upcome in a madigral partmoon
My love upright in a nightswoon
My love whose shoulders are sheen
Cartops to cop feeling for their chrome.
My love in limbery swimmer's layers
My love locuting to pithy players
And *above them the usual seabirds*

Sotted with faeryland's catchwords.
My love of the brim, my love of the coven,
The body or the buddy of my beloved . . .
I say the sea is beaming with your singing
Confounding the sailor with chest ringing.

One can hardly cope with the ocean,
One can hardly carp in the ocean
With Franklin's bits of almanac wisdom
The only distortion in the prism.
All I can hear in a hall of clatters
My love who paints the sundry smatters
Of something sublunary, something jabberwock
As all its strings it tunes to threstlecock.

CRUNK APPARENT

Marinely, let us melt in triplicate
Where moony amber fenestrates the seals
And gaudy gowns, done up like Juliet
Gainst etiquette roil their pederastic heels.
Sea-sotted divers, blubbery swimmers
Lipps crill in quintuplicate, well met blunt.
Doing dark country till the trough fairly shimmers
Gold teeth with lilac crush—crunk apparent.
Once gabardine now frill, knows no crunky
Cryptozoology, but rather tweets
And thrills, loose-lineated bacchardi,
Hennessey'll man my heartthrob on the streets—
     O slide your mic beneath my bonny mantle
     And hyphe me harder, angel, than I can handle.

OUR LOVE ISN'T DEPENDENT ON FOREIGN OIL

o swallow swallow
my <u>little</u> urchin
sleep in regress
peach with aplomb

no-one ever balks
at *behold*. I shall
break the clouds
with trying to—

kickinaw, crossing the potomac
with you in mind
crowing to the cows
to the deer eating seaweed

you—abbacromby catalogue
with no end
whatever syllables you require
I hasten to my lyre

tho the ardour of my ears
denies me nearly.
a spade is a heart
with a stem, unneighborly

paris discovers
sylvia's moonlet
binary asteroids, southpaws
complicateder than we thought

ganesha
with thir bowl of sweets
is not half so sweet
as when mandala'd

in the whorl of various
flesh you turn me in the wheel
and chrome me in the flesh
a delictation

devoutly to be wished
so let me have no tongue

except to speak of you
for where was once a puddle

is now a port, to stop
the dogs tangling to
shush the heathens' howling
for when the heart hearts

the head, the head bends
heartward, the heart
blooms skyward, all beat
and bleat way yonder

ANXIETY OF THE BULLFIGHT

I have been half-chlorinated by Love, a figure clowdily enwrapt,
my muse fucked by someone other than me, my patron leaving me
in the hall. My palm is luckily cool while I fret—fret—fret—then
whilst among the party I fret the onslaught with my lucky hand.
What Angel therewith could I transmew? But devils into stones, my
hand could shew . . . & the root anchorage you lit upon will be but
shadow in my sight—a little Narcoticke bower here, a little waltz
there. Which roote had otherwise me smote, I wonder in how seri-
ous a tone. Braggadoccio could wreake hisself in arms, & strum the
curious furies. But o, sad ladings of the bower—do not knights for
squiers take. There is no missus I am among.

COR, BLIMEY!

How could one pathos seke to wend itself
In prayse of centaurs or of dulcet ills
How would the flameater seek t'engulf
The flamethrower's geste, in thir own wet gills?
Similia similibus, same wants same
& yet one dips a pigtail in the ink
Or speaks barbrously in swete Cupid's name
As numbers maketh pig or pye turn pink.
Go stand on outcroppings of rock, go look
At penguins, twill only align you mor
With your desire—to despite the book
That seeks to name the thing wants naming: cor
Will I, nill I, that's neither here nor there
If one gives up the heart one has to spare.

SEA ALOE SONG

Sweets with sweets war not, joy delights in joy.
—SHAKESPEARE, Sonnet 8.2

Stellar sea cows, svelte manatees embrace
And lob their salty aloes each to each
While we graze greenly on the filtered rays
Fanned from their froth. I beg for you to teach
Me all the ways the Romans fucked, and how
Juventius, with honeyed eyes, would sit
In Catulle's lap, and lick his salty brow.
Of all the wooing words that ere were writ
Did Bernadette choose want for wit
Or skylark for a skylark's fond embrace?
Such salt would shame the sun to shade its rays
And cow fond lovers chomping at the bit.
   When they do buck and bray in sensate ardor
   Bottoming out the sea, fond sailor, fuck them harder.

SLOUGHING OFF THE GENTLEMANLY SPORTS

What makes that fox so grabby for the stars,
Begging like boys do? I meant to fully
Gild that lily, till less like virile Mars
It's clepd the pansiest of pansy,
The caducous calyx of a poppy.
Cuz, step into these arms where you belong
A coup at the prospect of this lording,
A gleam in the gloom with serpentine song—
The phosphorescent tide's mine to lavish upon.

O stop me at the very vestibule—
Before whom, and in what habit I speak
I watched them use their meat to call me fool.
Someone's cage is aching at the seams,
The noisome idle falls to dirty dreams—
Thus the flummoxed drunk of xem will coil
And I'll learn the real, or it'll learn me,
Making free with the Italian model
The single summer shower mano à mano.

The proverbial number of angels
That could've fit on the head of a pin
Are crying to the myriad angles,
This glassy labyrinth we happened in
Will not undo the errancer I've been.
Soon the swancrest, the feedcrest, my distress
Will feign to fuck the furlonged mannequin—
At what—punishing pace we undress
This crapshoot idée fixe and its yahoo mistress.

Fictive trees harsh the billow of my cape,
All kind of lovers crashed rubbernecking.
The fishes on the frontispiece were draped
In your leafy worded velocity.
You whisper, *London has no more fog for me*
To whit, my darksome peachpit! storms above
—A buckler to them that walks uprightly—
Will not enforce this porno hand from glove
Or diminish one jott my vegetable love.

NOTES

ADVICES

DISCIPULƎ AMORIS 5

Early 19th century sportswriter Pierce Egan coined the phrase 'the sweet science of bruising' to describe boxing.

ON HOW TO BLAZON YOUR LOVER 15

A boy in the stars with a hook in his hand.

———LARRY KEARNY

The face I wallow toward.

———ALICE FULTON

THE PERFECT LOVE POEM TUTORIAL 21

The Doldrums, also known as the 'horse latitutes,' pinpoints the place where the northeast and southeast tradewinds converge, and is notoriously dangers for sailors, with howling squalls and gigantic tropical waves. Sailors also tell 'hallucinating stories of this legendarily stagnant area, an otherworldly environment which is famous for being an area with no wind.'

I KNOCKED ALL TALES 23

I, the sultan of these vast purple props.

——TAFFY BEACON

Mister, here's a bag with all my money.

——JOHNNY CASH

ON NOT BEING ABLE TO PERCEIVE ANGELS 37

vegetable = 4 syllables

NUDISMS

RICKY MARTIN ON HOMOSEXUALITY 45

You can put my poster on the wall and think of it however you want.

——R.M.

RIME 49

Nothing else is.

——JOHN DONNE

YEAR OF THE MISFIT 50

They were here, here they were, there they went.
——Buffy the Vampire Slayer

LOWING THE LAY 69

After the Middle English romance *Amis and Amiloun*, c. 1300 (MS Auchinleck).

Roots in IE. [Indo-European] beginning with /l/ often indicate 'to move, withdraw, glide slowly, devour, lick, play, etc., in accordance with the function of /l/, produced by moving the tip of the tongue to the soft palate . . . Snowballing phonosemic overlap may be the source of so-called phonesthemes as the fl- in flee, fly, flow etc., and the -ash in bash, dash, gash etc.' (ALEXANDER JÓHANNESSON, *Origin of Language: Four Essays*).

NAUTITORIUM 71

Mummies are lovely but they are gone people.
——DALE SMITH

THE REAL, PURCHASED ON CREDIT, DOES NOT LIE BACK 74

Come, come, Nerissa, for I long to see
Quick Cupid's post that comes so mannerly.
——SHAKESPEARE, *Merchant of Venice* II.ix.99-100

ABOUT THE AUTHOR

Julian T. Brolaski is the author of *gowanus atropolis* (Ugly Duckling Presse, 2011) and the chapbooks *Hellish Death Monsters* (Spooky Press, 2001), *Letters to Hank Williams* (True West Press, 2003), *The Daily Usonian* (Atticus/Finch, 2004), *Madame Bovary's Diary* (Cy Press, 2005) and *A Buck in a Corridor* (flynpyntar, 2008/2009). Julian received a BA in Literature and Creative Writing from UC Santa Cruz, where xe studied with Nathaniel Mackey and Peter Gizzi, and an MFA in English and Creative Writing from Mills College, where xe studied with Elizabeth Willis and Stephen Ratcliffe. Julian is a PhD candidate in English at UC Berkeley, where xe studied with Lyn Hejinian and Robert Hass. Julian co-curated the New Brutalism poetry series in Oakland from 2003-2005 (with Cynthia Sailers) and the Holloway Poetry Series at UC Berkeley from 2004-2006 (with Lyn Hejinian and Anne Cheng). Julian has been an editor with Litmus Press since 2007. Xe is a poetry and essays editor of *Aufgabe* magazine and is also the co-editor (along w/ E. Tracy Grinnell and erica kaufman) of *NO GENDER: Reflections on the Life & Work of kari edwards* (Litmus Press/Belladonna Books, 2009). Julian lives in Brooklyn, teaches at the New School, curates Mongrel Vaudeville, and plays country and old time music with Juan & the Pines (www.reverbnation.com/juanandthepines) and the Invert Family Singers. New work is on the blog hermofwarsaw.

The state of the world calls out for poetry
to save it. LAWRENCE FERLINGHETTI

CITY LIGHTS SPOTLIGHT SHINES A LIGHT ON THE WEALTH
OF INNOVATIVE AMERICAN POETRY BEING WRITTEN TODAY.
WE PUBLISH ACCOMPLISHED FIGURES KNOWN IN THE
POETRY COMMUNITY AS WELL AS YOUNG EMERGING POETS,
USING THE CULTURAL VISIBILITY OF CITY LIGHTS TO BRING
THEIR WORK TO A WIDER AUDIENCE. IN DOING SO, WE ALSO
HOPE TO DRAW ATTENTION TO THOSE SMALL PRESSES
PUBLISHING SUCH AUTHORS. WITH CITY LIGHTS SPOTLIGHT,
WE WILL MAINTAIN OUR STANDARD OF INNOVATION AND
INCLUSIVENESS BY PUBLISHING HIGHLY ORIGINAL POETRY
FROM ACROSS THE CULTURAL SPECTRUM, REFLECTING
OUR LONGSTANDING COMMITMENT TO THIS MOST
ANCIENT AND STUBBORNLY ENDURING FORM OF ART.

CITY LIGHTS SPOTLIGHT

1

Norma Cole, *Where Shadows Will:*
Selected Poems 1988-2008

2

Anselm Berrigan, *Free Cell*

3

Andrew Joron, *Trance Archive:*
New and Selected Poems

4

Cedar Sigo, *Stranger in Town*

5

Will Alexander, *Compression & Purity*

6

Micah Ballard, *Waifs and Strays*

Printed in the USA
CPSIA information can be obtained
at www.ICGtesting.com
JSHW082222140824
68134JS00015B/676

9 780872 865815